OVERCOMING COVID-19 IN BHUTAN

LESSONS FROM COPING WITH THE PANDEMIC IN A TOURISM-DEPENDENT ECONOMY

DECEMBER 2021

ADB

ASIAN DEVELOPMENT BANK

Notes:
In this publication, "$" refers to United States dollars.

On the cover: **Local tourism in Bhutan.** Visitors walk up to the Tango Monastery in Thimphu, Bhutan (photo by Sonam Phuntsho for ADB).

Cover design by Rommel Marilla.

Contents

Tables and Figures

Abstract

Bhutan has carried out early and decisive measures to contain the spread of the coronavirus disease (COVID-19), including restrictions on tourists since March 2020. While this approach resulted in effectively containing the spread of COVID-19, it severely affected the economy with some sectors such as tourism and aviation coming to a virtual standstill. Given the country's limited resources and capacity to cope with a full-blown outbreak, such a trade-off was inevitable. Against such a backdrop, this brief discusses the Government of Bhutan's financial relief measures extended to the most affected people, as well as investment programs and other interventions, with a special focus on the tourism sector. The strategic thrust of interventions for the sector is based on striking the right balance between the immediate need to engage the economically displaced while simultaneously initiating major reforms and investments for a sustainable reopening.

Abbreviations

ADB	–	Asian Development Bank
COVID-19	–	coronavirus disease
FY	–	fiscal year
GDP	–	gross domestic product
SDF	–	sustainable development fee
TCB	–	Tourism Council of Bhutan

Currency Equivalents

Currency Unit	=	ngultrum (Nu)
Nu1.00	=	$0.0133
$1.00	=	Nu75.00

Background

1

Bhutan's economy grew at an annual average rate of 7% in 1998–2018. This growth was primarily driven by significant public investments in social infrastructure and hydropower, in addition to the steady performance of sectors such as tourism, construction, and manufacturing. Economic growth was supported by a strong adherence to macroeconomic prudence such as funding all recurrent expenditure through domestic revenue, maintaining adequate reserves, and channeling external sources of financing toward productive investment. Nevertheless, a slight deceleration (fiscal year [FY]2018: 3.8%; FY2019: 4.3%) was observed in 2018 and 2019, as illustrated in Table 1. During this period, growth has been largely driven by the tourism sector and, more broadly, services. The economy was anticipated to rebound with a growth of 5.2% in 2020 that was predicated on fiscal expansion as well as robust consumption growth. The coronavirus disease (COVID-19) pandemic has significantly altered these prospects with growth now expected to contract by –3.4% in 2021 from 0.9% in 2020. Preliminary forecast suggest that growth will pick up in 2021 to 3.7%, predicated on increased government investment.[1]

Table 1: Pre-COVID-19 Indicators

Item	Fiscal Year				
	2015	2016	2017	2018	2019
GDP growth (%, constant prices)	6.2	7.4	6.3	3.8	4.3
Inflation (CPI % change)	6.7	3.4	4.3	3.6	2.8
Current account balance (% of GDP)	(28.3)	(31.1)	(23.2)	(19.1)	(22.6)
Revenue and grants (% of GDP)	28.8	29.9	27.2	31.9	24.5
Expenditure and on lending (% of GDP)	29.3	32.0	31.9	32.2	27.4
Overall fiscal balance (deficit)	(1.5)	(1.1)	(3.4)	(0.3)	(2.2)
External public debt (% of GDP)	94.0	111.3	103.0	109.0	103.0
Gross international reserves ($ million)	958	1,119	1,104	1,111	1,065

( ) = negative, COVID-19 = coronavirus disease, CPI = consumer price index, GDP = gross domestic product.
Sources: Asian Development Bank estimates; Royal Government of Bhutan, Ministry of Finance; National Statistics Bureau.

---

[1] Asian Development Bank. 2021. *Asian Development Outlook 2021: Financing a Green and Inclusive Recovery*. Manila. http://dx.doi.org/10.22617/FLS210163-3.

The highly contagious nature of COVID-19 and the constraints of the health system in coping with a full-blown outbreak warranted stringent preventive action to minimize the spread of the disease. Against the recommended threshold of the World Health Organization (WHO) of 10 doctors and 40 nurses per 10,000 population, Bhutan's medical system, with only 4 doctors and 18 nurses per 10,000 population, is thinly stretched.[2] Upon detection of community transmission, the Government of Bhutan imposed two rounds of lockdown to break the transmission.[3]

These measures adversely affected economic activities across the country, including the crucial tourism sector. The sector is a significant part of Bhutan's economy, generating about $345 million in gross receipts and $23.4 million in direct government revenue through the sustainable development fee in 2019.[4] The sector is also very employment-intensive, thereby accentuating the impact of the pandemic. The hydropower sector, on the other hand, has provided significant respite with a 31% increase in generation due to the newly commissioned Mangdechu hydropower project and better hydrological flows in the same year.[5]

---

[2]   WHO. https://data.worldbank.org/ (accessed 8 January 2021).

[3]   The first nationwide lockdown was imposed on 11 August 2020 for 21 days and the second lockdown was imposed on 20 December 2020 for 25 days, but in the high-risk capital district, the lockdown lasted 40 days.

[4]   Royal Government of Bhutan, Tourism Council of Bhutan. 2020. *Bhutan Tourism Monitor 2019*. Thimphu. https://www.tourism.gov.bt/uploads/attachment_files/tcb_TNiOKGow_BTM%202019.pdf.

[5]   Royal Government of Bhutan, Royal Monetary Authority. 2021. *Monthly Statistical Bulletin*. January.

II Objective and Structure

This policy brief discusses the Government of Bhutan's response to the pandemic. More specifically, it assesses the financial relief measures extended to the most affected people, as well as investment programs and other interventions. Given the importance of tourism to Bhutan's economy and considering that it has suffered the most tangible impacts, this brief devotes special focus to the tourism sector.

III Socioeconomic Impacts

At the sector level, the first to feel the shockwaves due to movement restrictions were tour operators, hotels and restaurants, and transport companies. Further restrictions imposed on 22 March 2020, with the closure of surface entry points, resulted in significant supply-chain disruptions, especially of imports of goods and labor from India. The disruptions hit the construction sector, and the manufacturing sector also faced disruptions in the supply of raw material. In the construction sector, the initial workforce shortage due to restrictions was estimated at 14,495 workers. However, this is likely to have increased significantly as there has been an exodus of migrant labor back to India.[6] Furthermore, other precautionary measures such as physical distancing requirements also dampened demand in the retail and restaurant sector. It is estimated that household consumption alone declined by 24% coupled with a 3% decline in private investment.[7]

The directly affected sectors such as tourism have multiple linkages to the rest of the economy: in addition to being employment-intensive, they contribute tax revenue as well as convertible currency. Convertible currency receipts from international arrivals was projected to contribute $92 million in 2020. In the first quarter of the year prior to the detection of the first case, convertible currency receipts were recorded at $10.14 million. Following the restrictions, it is estimated that nearly $82 million has been forgone.[8] On the employment front, an estimated 11,798 employees in the tourism and allied sectors have been directly affected. The hotels and restaurant sector, in particular, have a disproportionately large share of unskilled female employees.

Further losses in the form of sales taxes and corporate income taxes from other sectors are weakening the revenue stream. Considering that average domestic spending accounts for 27.4% of gross domestic product (GDP), an inevitable weakening in the government's fiscal position will reinforce weak aggregate demand. Revised estimates for the fiscal year 2020 alone highlight a 9% decline in domestic revenue compared to initial projections.[9] Consequently, the fiscal deficit is expected to widen to 6.18% of GDP in 2021 compared to 3.0% of GDP for 2020 (footnote 9). The impact for the fiscal year 2021 is more pronounced with a steep decline in domestic revenue of 23% contributing to a further widening of the fiscal deficit to 7.4% of GDP.

---

[6] Royal Government of Bhutan. 2020. Economic Contingency Plan Phase I.
[7] Royal Government of Bhutan, Prime Minister's Office. 2020. State of the Nation Address.
[8] M. B. Subba. 2021. Unprecedented Setbacks for Economy. *Kuensel*. 13 February. https://kuenselonline.com/unprecedented-setbacks-for-economy/.
[9] Royal Government of Bhutan, Ministry of Finance. 2020. National Budget Report 2020–2021.

The pandemic has also warranted a reprioritization of the government's development activities. Considering that growth was expected to be supported by a 51% elevation in capital expenditure, the supply disruptions are already impeding infrastructure expansion and other development spending, thereby depressing longer-term growth prospects as well. In the first half of FY2021, only about 6.2% of the total allocation for capital works had been used due to implementation challenges arising from labor and material shortages.

The implications for the finance sector are also apparent. The tourism and service sector accounts for 24% of total outstanding credit. With a freeze in business, defaults are imminent, although for now, interest waivers are providing relief to borrowers. Other sectors within services such as construction, with the contractors, are under stress as well. With the recent sharp increase in nonperforming loans to 16%, financial indicators are likely to further breach macro-prudential thresholds.

As a result of the rise in imported and domestic food prices, the year-on-year inflation reached a 7-year high in the third quarter of 2020. Consumer price index (CPI) inflation averaged just above 2% in the 6 months before the first case was detected in March.[10] In August, it grew to 7.67% (Figure 1). This is mainly due to an increase in the prices of food and non-alcoholic beverages (15.34%), and alcoholic beverages and betel nuts (9%). Since there are anticipated supply chain disruptions in food production into the medium term, food prices are also expected to rise over this period.

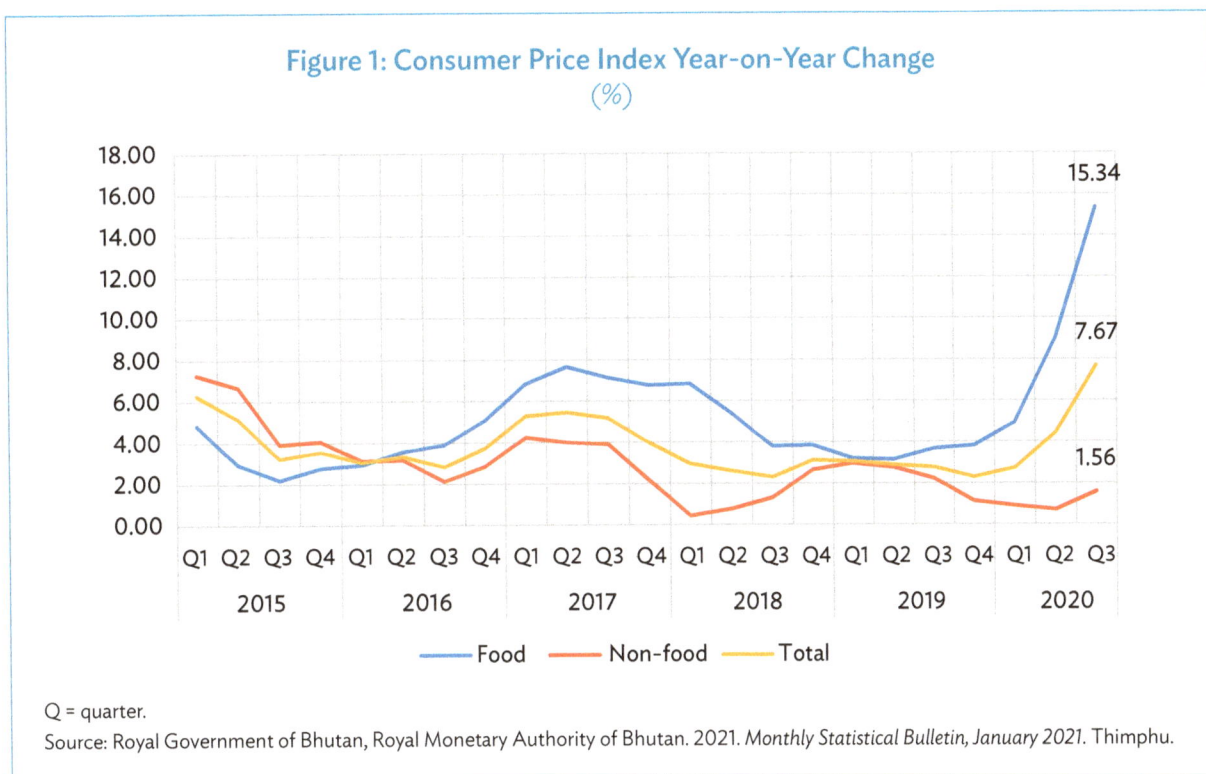

Figure 1: Consumer Price Index Year-on-Year Change
(%)

Q = quarter.
Source: Royal Government of Bhutan, Royal Monetary Authority of Bhutan. 2021. *Monthly Statistical Bulletin, January 2021*. Thimphu.

---

[10]   Royal Government of Bhutan, Royal Monetary Authority of Bhutan. 2021. *Monthly Statistical Bulletin*, January 2021. Thimphu.

While these preventive measures may have dampened growth, some level of economic activity was still possible. However, the two subsequent lockdowns that were imposed for 46 days brought the entire economy to a standstill. During the second lockdown, the epicenters of the outbreak were Thimphu and Paro, two critically important centers of economic activities. Given the extent of the outbreak, the lockdown for Thimphu and Paro were extended by 2 more weeks in addition to 26 days despite relaxations in other districts. Besides the economic impacts, 223 cases of gender-based violence were reported during the protracted lockdown.[11]

[11]   Y. Lhaden. 2021. Gender-Based Violence Spikes 53.5% in 2020. *Kuensel*.19 March. https://kuenselonline.com/gender-based-violence-spikes-53-5-percent-in-2020/.

IV Immediate Interventions— Proactive and Decisive Public Health Responses

Upon detection of the first case, a restriction on the entry of foreigners by air was imposed. The government was proactive in formulating the National Preparedness and Response Plan (NPRP) for COVID-19 "with the objective to enhance the health sector's capacity in surveillance, early detection, control and prevention, response, and recovery from [the] COVID-19 outbreak in the country."[12] Early responses also included the establishment of designated isolation wards in national and regional hospitals for COVID-19 positive patients. Across Bhutan, flu clinics were set up to detect strains of the virus.[13] The plan is flexible with reviews and updates undertaken as and when required by the Technical Advisory Group (TAG) of the Ministry of Health.

Figure 2: National Situational Update, as of 30 September 2021

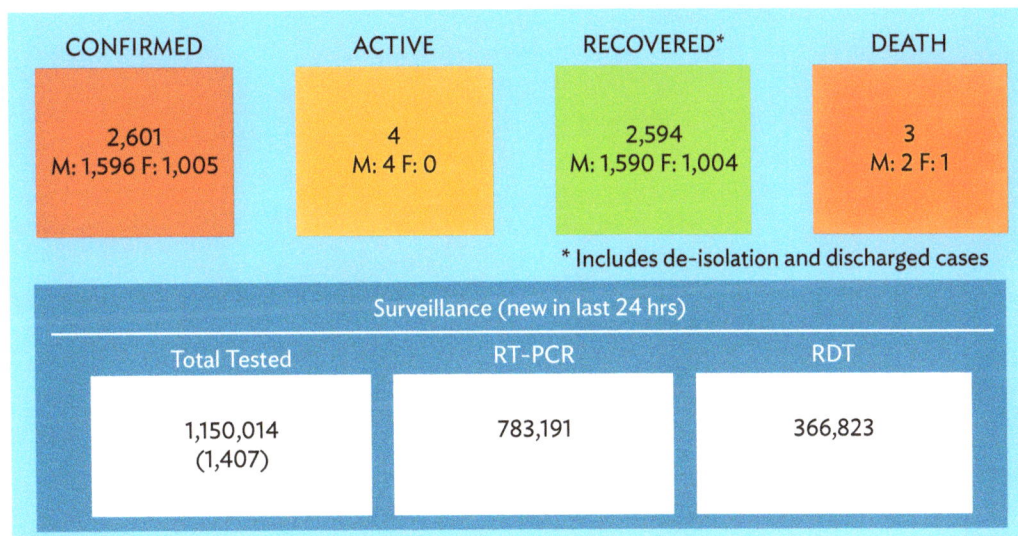

CONFIRMED	ACTIVE	RECOVERED*	DEATH
2,601 M: 1,596 F: 1,005	4 M: 4 F: 0	2,594 M: 1,590 F: 1,004	3 M: 2 F: 1

* Includes de-isolation and discharged cases

Surveillance (new in last 24 hrs)		
Total Tested	RT-PCR	RDT
1,150,014 (1,407)	783,191	366,823

F = female, M = male.

Note: RT-PCR (reverse transcription polymerase chain reaction) and RDT (rapid diagnostic test) are types of tests to detect coronavirus disease (COVID-19).

Source: Royal Government of Bhutan, Ministry of Health. COVID-19 Government Portal.

---

12   Royal Government of Bhutan, Ministry of Health. 2020. National Preparedness and Response Plan for Outbreak of Novel Coronavirus. Thimphu. 16 March. http://www.moh.gov.bt/wp-content/uploads/ict-files/2020/01/National-Preparedness-and-Response-Plan-4th-ed.pdf.

13   L. Tshering. 2020. State of the Nation. Fourth Session: The Third Parliament of Bhutan. 12 December. https://www.nab.gov.bt/assets/uploads/images/news/2020/State_of_the_Nation_2020.pdf.

The emphasis on prevention and detection is evident in Bhutan's testing rates (Figure 2). The country has recorded one of the highest per capita reverse transcription polymerase chain reaction (RT-PCR) testing rates in South Asia at 1,150,014 tests per million inhabitants as of 30 September 2021.[14] Overall, 783,191 RT-PCR and 366,823 rapid diagnostic tests (RDT) have been administered. Besides two periods of local transmission, the country has managed to achieve its preventive objectives thus far. The nationwide lockdowns have also been effective in detecting and isolating cases to break the transmission. During the 21 days after the first lockdown was imposed, the number of detected cases nearly doubled (Figure 3). This detection was crucial in preventing further spread. In the second lockdown, the number of cases detected jumped 72% from a larger base of 446 to 767 in a span of 20 days. Bhutan also mourned its first fatality during this period.

Given the resource constraints and limited health facilities—both infrastructure and personnel—the institutional capacity of the country could be overwhelmed in the event of a full-blown outbreak. Indeed, other areas of priority are coming under pressure as well, such as the provision of essential services, revenue generation, and education. As observed with the second outbreak, which was more significant in magnitude and required extended lockdowns in two critical hubs, the impacts are multidimensional.

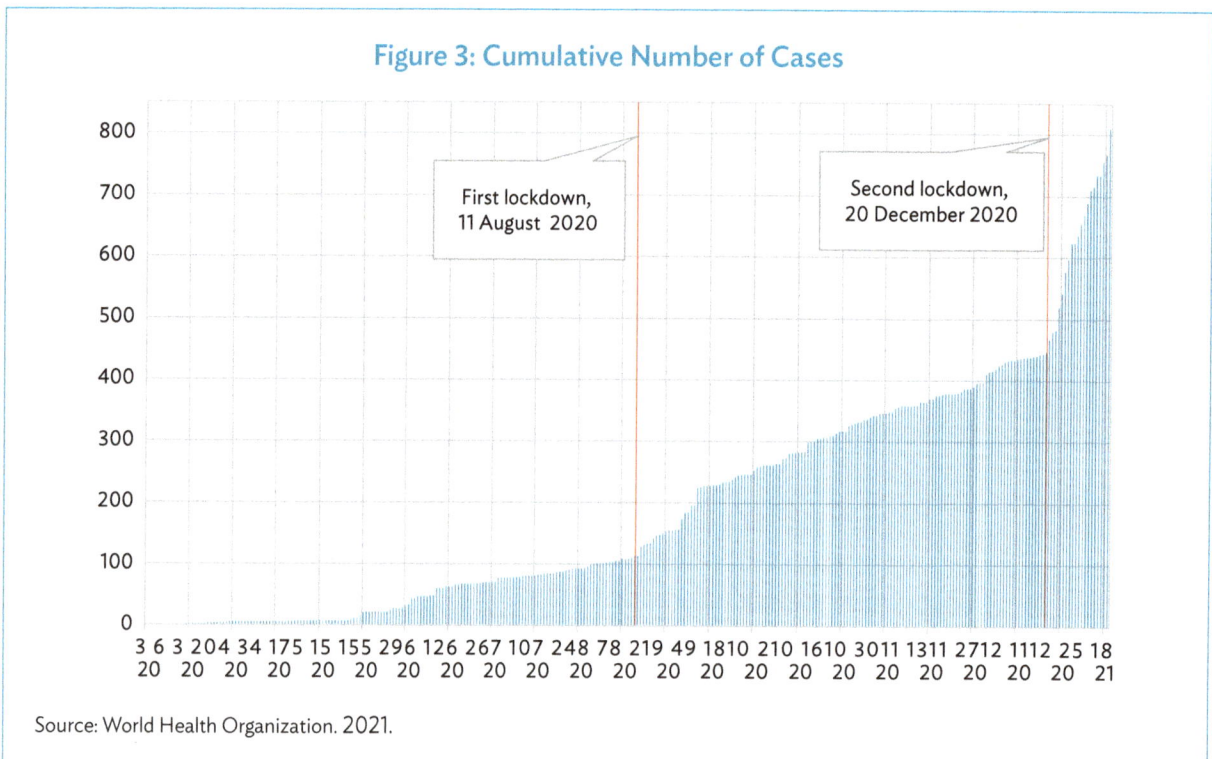

Figure 3: Cumulative Number of Cases

First lockdown, 11 August 2020

Second lockdown, 20 December 2020

Source: World Health Organization. 2021.

---

[14] This is estimated for a population of 748,931.

As a society characterized by extended family households and high social interactions, the potential severity of contagion is extremely high. For instance, the severity of the second outbreak has been attributed to the annual family and social gatherings that take place toward the end of the year. Accordingly, the highest standards of preparedness and preventive measures have been pursued.[15] This has included a mandatory quarantine of 21 days for all returning citizens as well as expatriates. In the absence of adequate hospital accommodation, the government has resorted to using the facilities of unutilized hotel rooms at negotiated rates. Between March 2020 and November 2020, 24,148 people underwent the government-funded mandatory quarantine period. The Ministry of Health was provided with an initial budget of Nu1.0 billion ($13.33 million) for prevention, containment, and treatment from April to August 2020. Furthermore, an additional Nu2.0 billion ($26.66 million) was allocated for heath-related response measures in preparation for a worst-case scenario. This has facilitated certain unprecedented actions. For instance, hospitals carried out fast-track recruitment of about 140 doctors, nurses, and technicians to help manage the pandemic (footnote 13).

To facilitate movement within the country while also observing caution, passenger registration is mandatory for effective contact tracing. An online portal has been launched to minimize administrative burden while keeping record of the movement of people across districts. For instance, through contact tracing for the second outbreak, it was estimated that 38,000 people traveled between 7 December and 20 December 2020.

The government has also adopted a more differentiated approach that includes demarcating zones and allowing activities based on the status of each location. This has allowed some level of economic activity to continue.

---

[15]   World Health Organization. 2020. "Invest in Preparedness"– Health Emergency Readiness Lessons From Bhutan. 27 November. https://www.who.int/news-room/feature-stories/detail/invest-in-preparedness-health-emergency-readiness-lessons-from-bhutan.

V | Socioeconomic Interventions— The Comprehensive National Response to COVID-19

The Nu30 billion (approximately $400 million) Comprehensive National Response was launched on 10 April 2020 to address the immediate socioeconomic challenges of the COVID-19 pandemic while initiating efforts to address longer-term priorities. These responses were also complemented by front-loading prioritized development activities from the 12th Five-Year Plan (2018–2023) to stimulate economic activity by offsetting the decline in private sector demand. This has resulted in a reallocation of 32% of the capital outlay for the 12th Five-Year Plan to FY2021. On the financing side, the government also issued its first sovereign bond of Nu3 billion at a coupon rate of 6.5%, which was done to support economic recovery from the pandemic and diversify financial sources.[16] To ensure an inclusive response, three overarching interventions are being implemented:

(i) A social relief grant for individuals directly affected by the pandemic for 8 months (April–December 2020) had been disbursed, which was further extended to 2021. The grants that range from Nu7,000 to Nu12,000 ($93–$160) are disbursed monthly. It has been recorded that 34,384 beneficiaries have received the stipend at least once.[17] The total amount dispensed as on 30 September 2021 was Nu3,201 million ($46.68).

Table 2: Social Relief Beneficiaries

Recipients by Number of Months Supported	Male	Female	Total
One	3,600	2,914	6,514
Two	1,792	1,507	3,299
Three	3,106	2,316	5,422
Four	2,776	1,819	4,595
Five	1,020	1,185	2,205
Six	735	798	1,533
Seven	1,484	1,601	3,085
Eight	3,997	3,734	7,731
Total	18,510	15,874	34,384

Source: T. Palden. 2020. Druk Gyalpo's Kidu Extended for the Most Needy. *Kuensel*. 25 December.

16 M. B. Subba. 2020. Bhutan's First Government Bond, Worth Nu 3B, Well-Received. *Kuensel*. 26 September. https://kuenselonline.com/bhutans-first-govt-bond-worth-nu-3b-well-received/.

17 T. Palden. 2020. Druk Gyalpo's Kidu Extended for the Most Needy. *Kuensel*. 25 December. https://kuenselonline.com/druk-gyalpos-relief-kidu-extended-for-the-most-needy/.

(ii)   An immediate monetary measure to inject liquidity included the reduction in Cash Reserve Ratio from 10% to 9% on 17 March 2020. This was further reduced to 7% on 27 April 2020, to enable lending which resulted in a liquidity release equivalent to Nu4,108 million ($54.77 million). Additional measures include (a) full waiver of interest and a repayment deferment for 6 months for all businesses, followed by a partial waiver of interest and a repayment deferment for an additional 6 months; (b) subsidized working capital at a preferential rate of 5%; (c) extension of gestation period for ongoing projects by 3 months (extendable by another 3 months); (d) working capital through the National Cottage and Small Industries (CSI) Bank to CSIs at an interest rate of 4% for a period of 3 months (extendable by another 3 months); and (e) microloans through CSI Bank loans up to a ceiling of Nu0.5 million at an interest rate of 2% for a period of 3 months (extendable by another 3 months). On the fiscal front, a deferment of business and corporate income taxes, and sales tax for businesses, and customs duty on essential imports was granted. The National Credit Guarantee Scheme was launched for a coverage of Nu3 billion. The scheme will be providing cottage and small industries with collateral-free loans. Under this scheme, the government guarantees a portion of the loans availed for establishing a viable business in return for a 10% equity with start-ups eligible for 100% debt financing. Larger businesses are also eligible for loan financing up to 50% or Nu30 million, whichever is larger.[18]

(iii) The Economic Contingency Plan is a set of targeted measures involving specific activities to productively engage economically displaced people.[19] These targeted interventions are being implemented through three thrust areas with a total outlay of Nu4,932 million ($65.76 million). The three thrust areas are summarized below with the tourism intervention discussed in further detail in the next section:

(a) **Tourism resilience.** The pandemic provides a unique platform to address longer-term policy issues while improving infrastructure and diversifying the sector's product base by engaging the economically displaced in the medium term. The budget to carry out these activities is Nu232 million ($3.09 million).

(b) **Food self-sufficiency and nutrition security.** The agriculture sector contingency plan seeks to boost agriculture and livestock production by providing a range of support measures across the value chain that include technical assistance and funding for marketing, value addition, and providing year-round connectivity and road access (footnote 19). Nu3,605 million ($48.06 million) has been budgeted for these activities.

(c) **Build Bhutan Project.** This project seeks to institute a range of strategies to meet the labor demand, especially that of skilled workers by engaging the displaced (footnote 19). In addition to addressing the immediate shortage of workers, the project is geared toward addressing other longer-term objectives in the industry such as specialization and professionalization. A total of Nu1,040 million ($13.86 million) has been budgeted for the project.

---

[18]   Royal Government of Bhutan, National Credit Guarantee Scheme. http://www.ncgs.gov.bt/.
[19]   Royal Government of Bhutan. 2020. *Economic Contingency Plan—Redesigning Development: Attaining Greater Heights.* https://www.cabinet.gov.bt/wp-content/uploads/2020/07/ECP-2020.pdf.

Figure 4: The Government of Bhutan's Socioeconomic Response

```
                    Comprehensive
                    National Response
                    to COVID-19

   Social relief grant    Monetary and fiscal      Economic
                          interventions            Contingency Plan

                          Interest waiver          Food self-sufficiency
                                                   and nutrition
                                                   security

                          Concessional             Tourism resilience
                          working capital loan

                          National Credit          Build Bhutan Project
                          Guarantee Scheme
```

COVID-19 = coronavirus disease.
Source: Asian Development Bank.

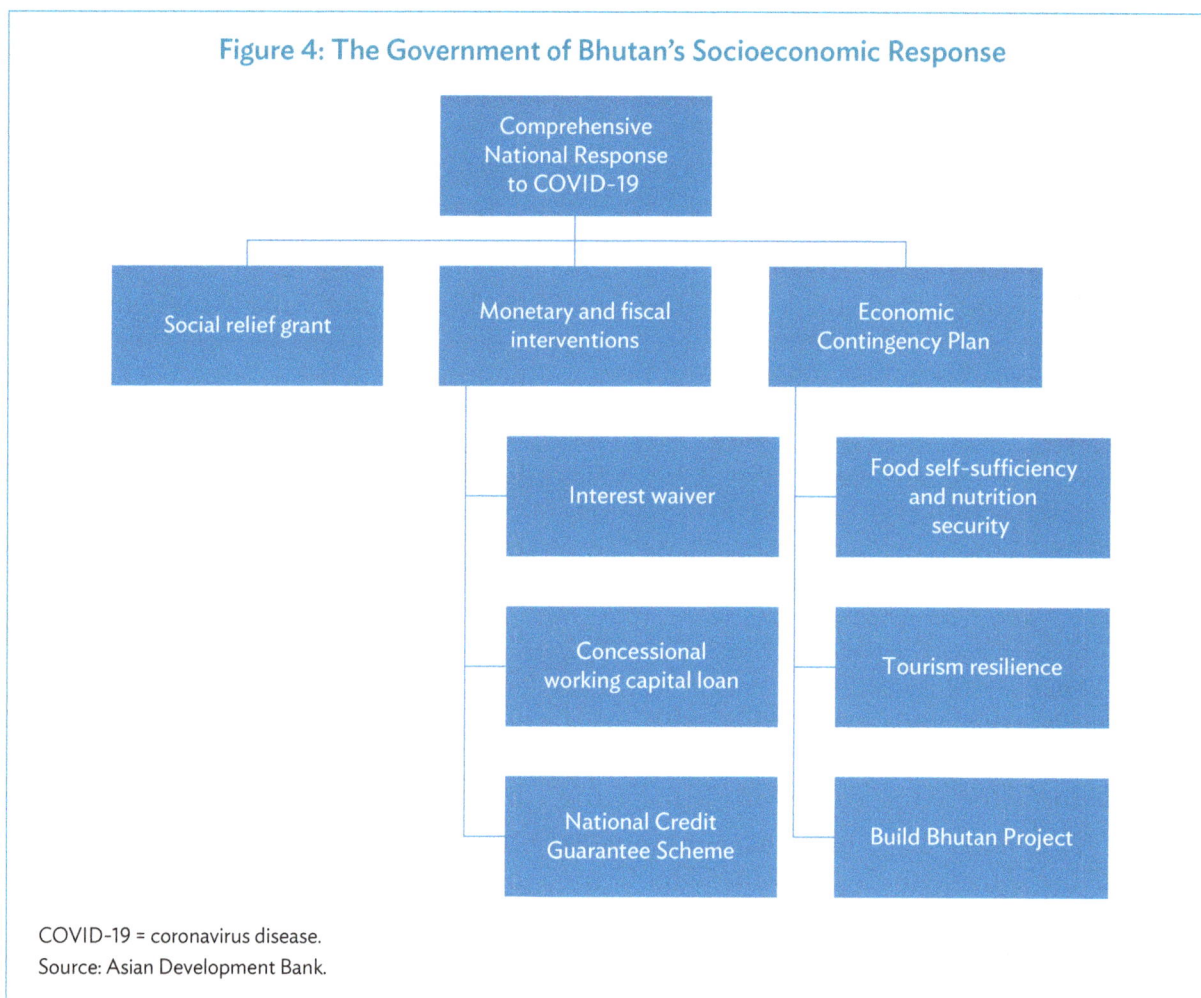

The government has depended on a variety of sources to raise funding for these response measures, including the sale of domestic bonds and assistance from development partners such as the Asian Development Bank (ADB) under the Countercyclical Support Facility for the COVID-19 Active Response and Expenditure Support (CARES) program.[20] On 4 May 2020, ADB approved a loan of $20 million with the full amount disbursed effectively. The CARES program is intended to provide the government additional fiscal space to address critical public health needs while also managing the economic downturn.

More specifically, the program contributes to the following impacts: (i) the adverse consequences of COVID-19 on the economy and livelihood of the vulnerable population mitigated, and (ii) public health responses against infectious diseases strengthened. The associated outcomes are: (i) immediate socioeconomic conditions improved and (ii) critical public health and safety requirements strengthened. These will be achieved through three outputs: (i) financial relief for distressed individuals implemented, (ii) COVID-19 response expenditures strengthened, and (iii) economic stimulus for productive sectors delivered.

---

[20]   ADB. Bhutan: COVID-19 Active Response and Expenditure Support Program. https://www.adb.org/projects/54183-001/main.

Special Focus—Strengthening Tourism for Recovery and Resilience

VI

The tourism sector is strategic for Bhutan on multiple fronts. In the years prior to the pandemic, the sector was a strong driver of growth that also facilitated the growth of auxiliary sectors such as transport, hotels and accommodations, and handicrafts. Tourism inflows in the last 5 years grew at a near compounded annual average of 30% (Figure 5).

The sector is also the largest generator of convertible currency in addition to its employment intensive nature with multiple linkages to other sectors such as accommodation, transportation, and many more. For instance, it is estimated that during the pandemic, 50,737 people from the tourism sector have been affected directly and indirectly. A rapid socioeconomic assessment conducted by the United Nations Development Programme and the National Statistics Bureau involved the designing of a Multidimensional Vulnerability Index for Tourism (MVI-T) which identified eight deprivations: (i) income loss, (ii) coping strategy, (iii) loss of livelihood, (iv) food security, (v) limited savings, (vi) indebtedness, (vii) vulnerable household members, and (viii) tourism dependence. Based on

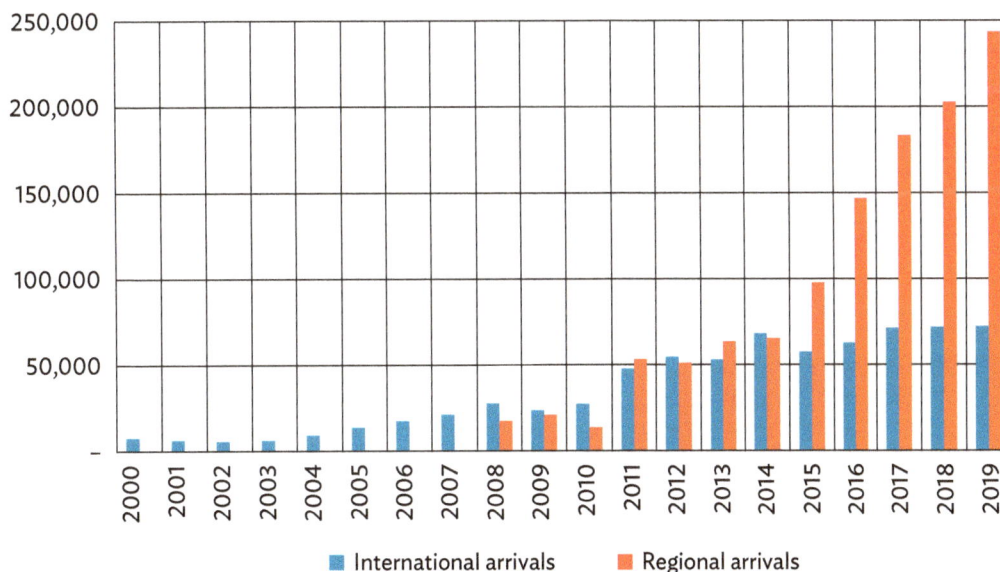

Figure 5: Tourism Arrivals

Source: Royal Government of Bhutan, Tourism Council of Bhutan. 2020. *Bhutan Tourism Monitor 2019*.

the MVI-T, over 80% of respondents of the survey reported facing three or more deprivations simultaneously.[21] It was reported that almost one-third of the 1,285 surveyed had lost their jobs or were placed on leave without pay (footnote 21).

The direct reduction in tourism earnings is estimated at 40% for FY2020 and 100% for FY2021 as international tourism has not yet resumed as of September 2021. On a calendar year basis, gross receipts fell by 92% to $19.84 million in 2020, from $225.87 million in 2019. Direct revenue is estimated to have dropped by 90.4% to $2.63 million in 2020, from $27.23 million in 2019.[22]

While the pandemic has resulted in heavy socioeconomic costs, the situation also presents a unique opportunity to initiate much-needed reforms in a carefully contained context. Indeed, there is an appetite for reform at the moment and many measures to expedite processes and decision-making are already offering insights on designing effective interventions and regulations. Moreover, the imperative to increasingly digitize is also being accelerated on a widespread scale.

Thus far, Bhutan's overarching policy of "high value, low volume tourism" has provided a strong framework in ensuring a balance between economic, social, and environmental outcomes. However, even before the onslaught of the pandemic, there were many challenges confronting the sector. Tourism is still characterized by seasonality, geographic inequities, a limited range of packages, and negligible increases in spend per tourists, warranting significant interventions. More recently, the number of high-end international tourists has stagnated while an influx of regional tourists has raised alarm as it undermines the "high value, low volume" policy stance of the nation.

Prior to the pandemic, a regulatory change in the form of the Sustainable Development Fee for regional tourists was anticipated to significantly impact the industry.[23] There were two divergent outlooks. While it was expected that the fee would arrest the steep increase in budget regional tourists, a concern was the downturn of many businesses that had built dependence on this new segment of customers. However, due to the onset of the pandemic and the resulting closure of tourism, the government is unable to assess the impacts.

Given the centrality of the sector, it is not surprising that tourism is one of the three domains of focus for the government's response to the pandemic. While an evaluation of the effectiveness of interventions at this point is not possible as some interventions are still under implementation, an assessment of the approach and intent is provided in the next section.

Bhutan's interventions in the tourism sector present a two-pronged approach. This includes (i) promoting domestic tourism in the immediate term to sustain some level of activity, and (ii) strengthening the foundations of the sector to revive and grow the international tourist segment. For the second approach, there are two sets of interventions as well. One intervention focuses on supply-side infrastructure and human resource improvements by engaging the economically displayed, while the other focuses on the regulatory and policy framework.

---

[21]   Royal Government of Bhutan, National Statistics Bureau and United Nations Development Programme. 2020. *Rapid Socio-Economic Impact Assessment of COVID-19 on Bhutan's Tourism Sector: An Analysis of the Vulnerability of Individuals, Households and Businesses Engaged in the Tourism Sector.* May. https://www.bt.undp.org/content/bhutan/en/home/library/environment_energy/rapid-socio-economic-impact-assessment-of-covid-19-on-bhutan-s-t.html.

[22]   Royal Government of Bhutan, Prime Minister's Office. 2020. State of the Nation Address.

[23]   Royal Government of Bhutan, Tourism Council of Bhutan. 2020. *Tourism Levy Act of Bhutan.* Thimphu.

Economic Contingency Plan: Tourism Resilience

While the Tourism Council of Bhutan (TCB) already had a series of interventions in the pipeline, most notably the Tourism Flagship Program, the Economic Contingency Plan (ECP) was formulated to focus on the sector in response to the pandemic. Harnessing the synergies between the flagship program's content and the urgency of the ECP, the TCB was able to use 78% of the allocated funds of the flagship program for 2020.

The interventions were formulated to address the following objectives (footnote 19):

(i)   Engaging the economically displaced.
(ii) Professionalizing employees in the tourism sector, and identifying new tourism products and providing a facelift for tourism infrastructure as part of an engagement program for economically displaced employees.
(iii) Strengthening tourism governance.
(iv) Maintaining and promoting Bhutan's image as an exclusive high-end and sustainable tourism destination.

Toward these objectives, interventions were formulated under four broad categories (footnote 19).

(i)   **Infrastructure and product development.** Bhutan faces an infrastructure deficit across many domains. To operate as a high-end tourist destination, an adequate and reliable infrastructure network is critical. However, the last time major infrastructure works such as the widening of the East–West highway took place, it created severe inconvenience for tourists traveling across the country. The pandemic has provided a period of recess for the sector to carry out significant expansion and consolidation of infrastructure. It is likely that activities included upgrading of tourist destinations and monuments. Additionally, new trails, quality roadside amenities, campsites, and various revamping works are needed. The infrastructure and product development sites were identified based on their local and tourist popularity.

It is becoming increasingly clear that the limited range of tourism products has also reduced the average length of stay of tourists and, consequently, has limited gross receipts. The regional imbalance in tourism is also attributable to a lack of marketable products in other locations besides the more popular destinations of Western and Central Bhutan. Therefore, preparatory works for the launch of cultural and highland festivals in the eastern districts of Trashigang, Trashiyangtse, and Lhuentse have been completed. New cultural destinations are being explored in Haa, and infrastructure for visitors have been enhanced in Gasa.

(ii) **Training and re-skilling.** The tourism sector's human resources, guides in particular, are indispensable given the regulatory requirement for tourists to be escorted by certified guides. While there has been a steady flow of trained employees into the tourism industry, the present recess provides an opportunity for existing employees to deepen, diversify, or acquire new skills. Notwithstanding the healthy supply of bilingual guides, they only possess a set of general skills with limited specialization and professional progression. Therefore, the capacity building areas have been identified based on emerging trends in the tourism industry and are being pursued in collaboration with stakeholders. These areas include

(a) handicrafts and souvenir production,
(b) hotel assessment,
(c) wellness and spa (Sowa Rigpa),

(d) upgrading the guide course, and

(e) advanced food production.

Thus far, over 135 displaced persons have participated in the programs and an additional 60 craftspeople have been trained.

(iii) **Survey and studies.** It is clear that certain policy decisions have been impeded by a lack of information. For instance, a central question that still lacks clarity is the definition of Bhutan's tourism policy slogan "High value, low volume." While the "high value" element is operationalized through the minimum daily package rate, a threshold for the "low volume" aspiration has yet to be identified as it requires an understanding of the carrying capacity of the existing infrastructure and tourist attractions. Similarly, an attempt to promote regionally balanced tourism also requires an understanding of the potential of each district. The standstill in the sector provides a unique opportunity to acquire updated information. These will also inform future interventions. Two activities in particular are being undertaken (footnote 19).

(a) **Tourism resource inventory.** This project involves building a comprehensive database encompassing tourist attractions, products, services, and infrastructure at various locations. This would serve as a valuable tool and reference for both tour operators and tourists, and enable the design of additional and customizable packages. The earlier resource inventory survey conducted in 2005 has not been updated and is not comprehensive. The project aims to build on the previous survey by capturing the historical details and significance of each tourism resource. The questionnaires for the survey have been finalized and the survey will be undertaken shortly.

(b) **Updated Google Street View imagery.** Google Maps have become an instrumental tool for travelers who use it to explore destinations and businesses that use it as a platform to attract new clients. The feature was launched in Bhutan in 2014 with no updates since then despite significant changes in the urban landscape. The Google Street View initiative has thus far updated the street view of all 20 districts with the latest images. Through Google Maps and Google Earth, the updated imagery will provide tourists with easy access to information, including cultural, religious, and heritage attractions; nature-based attractions; recreations and special events.

(iv) **Waste management.** The alarming increase in solid waste is a threat to Bhutan's image as a pristine high-end destination. Indeed, what is clear is that it is not necessarily the volume of waste, but its management that needs to be addressed. Therefore, this activity focuses on managing waste along the most frequented trekking routes and tourist hot spots through cleaning, advocacy, and awareness programs on waste. Thus far, 20 popular tourist sites have benefited from the campaign.

With a total budget allocation of Nu213.78 million, the programs were planned for two phases (Phase I from April to June 2020, and Phase II from July to December 2020) (footnote 19). Thus far, the program has engaged 1,330 displaced employees from the sector, more than the targeted number of 1,000.

Tourism Reforms

Besides immediate supply-side investments and measures, the standstill has also provided a platform to assess the policy environment and introduce governance and operational reforms. The following programs relating to governance and operations are being pursued to prepare the sector for reopening once the pandemic abates.

(i)   **Readiness to implement sustainable development fee.** The sustainable development fee (SDF) for regional tourists was a hallmark regulation imposed to manage the recent influx of regional tourists. While the regulation was passed, there were mixed expectations and one of the concerns was the lack of clarity in implementing it. The suspension of tourism indefinitely has provided time to develop a robust and seamless set of guidelines. Toward this, an interim standard operating protocol (SOP) for SDF has been drafted and will be implemented until the full Guideline for Management of Regional Tourism is rolled out as part of the National Tourism Policy.[24] This will facilitate and guide the payment of SDF by regional tourists while also clearly delineating the roles and responsibilities of stakeholders in terms of the SDF. This is also intended to enhance professionalism and service delivery for regional tourists. The sensitization and approval of guidelines on the management of regional tourism have been completed by all relevant stakeholders, including embassies and missions. The principle behind this is to ensure uniformity in application of the "high value, low volume" policy by extending the same level of international service to regional tourists as well.

(ii) **New entry points.** Bhutan continues to face difficulty in ensuring a more proportional distribution of tourists regionally despite various incentives offered, such as waiver of the SDF for certain locations. In fact, 80% of tourists are still concentrated in the five districts of Paro, Thimphu, Punakha, Wangdue Phodrang, and Bumthang (Figure 6). In addition to the previously cited reasons, this is also due to the limited aviation entry points and underdeveloped internal road network. To prepare for the reopening of the sector and to facilitate a regionally balanced spread of tourists across the country, especially in the southern foothills with favorable weather conditions in winter, two new entry points with integrated check-post facilities are being set up at Gelephu and Samdrup Jongkhar (footnote 24). These new entry points are also critical considering the limited aviation entry points.

(iii) **Assessment of budget hotels.** The recently approved SDF necessitates regional tourists to stay in certified hotels. The TCB is conducting a nationwide survey of currently uncertified hotels for possible certification. Displaced tour guides, hotel staff, and tour operations staff are conducting the survey (footnote 24). Thus far, 322 budget hotels nationwide have been assessed.

(iv) **Systems integration.** Leveraging digital technology across domains such as visa application, bookings, and payment is a priority. The tourism sector relies on over five systems, including Tashel Visa Online and costing system, which are currently isolated, resulting in loopholes. The activity proposes integration of these systems to ease processes such as transferring of tour payments and refunds. The TCB, in collaboration with the banks, is working to integrate the payment aggregator of the respective banks with the tashel system by using the relevant application programming interface. This will automate the process of manually updating credit advice from the banks, while also significantly reducing turnaround time.

---

24   Y. Tshedup. 2020. Govt. To Set Up S/Jongkhar and Gelephu as Tourist Entry Points. *Kuensel*. 2 July. https://kuenselonline.com/govt-to-set-up-s-jongkhar-and-gelephu-as-tourist-entry-points/.

Figure 6: Regional Imbalance of Visitors, 2019

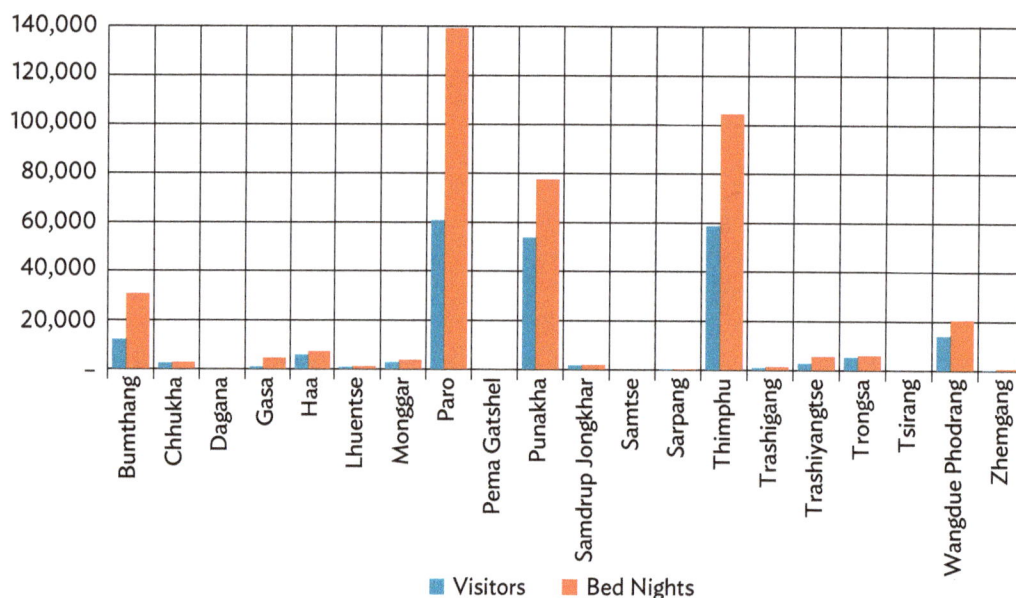

Source: Royal Government of Bhutan, Tourism Council of Bhutan. 2019. *Bhutan Tourism Monitor 2019*. Thimphu.

(v) **Regulatory frameworks.** In addition to physical infrastructure, institutional infrastructure plays an instrumental role. A range of regulations is being reviewed while other regulations are being introduced in preparation for reopening. Some of these include the formulation of Tourism Levy Rules and Regulation; the development of Guidelines for the Development of Luxury Tented Accommodations; the review and refinement of the draft criteria for the Assessment and Certification of Tented Accommodation; and the development of proposals on the management of non-star rated (budget) hotels and unlicensed accommodations. These will be complemented by the critical task of streamlining permit and visa issuances (footnote 13).

(vi) **Nation branding.** The pandemic will require a significant advertising drive to attract hesitant tourists once travel resumes. To position Bhutan for a post-pandemic world, several initiatives are already underway. The recently initiated Bhutan Tourism Dialogue Series provides a consultative platform for tourism stakeholders to discuss issues and strategies. Most prominently, a 60-second promotional video was aired on CNN. A more elaborate communication campaign, "Unlock Happiness," has been produced to position Bhutan as the "number one destination" for a safe and unique travel experience among targeted audiences (footnote 13).

Domestic Tourism Offers Some Respite

While these measures have been focused on strengthening the Bhutan asset stock and ecosystem of tourism, domestic tourism has been an overlooked market segment. Harnessing the synergy between domestic tourism and pilgrimage is an underexplored opportunity, especially for the retired and elderly population. Even as early as 2015, it was estimated that 100,000 Bhutanese traveled annually on pilgrimage and spent Nu1.5 billion.[25] More recent surveys, such as the Domestic and Outbound Tourism Survey 2019 (Figure 7), indicate that out of 41,163 outbound tourists, 45% were pilgrims mostly headed to India.[26] A distinguishing feature of tourists traveling for pilgrimage is their high average length of stay. It is further estimated that outbound tourists expended close to Nu1.8 billion, out of which pilgrimage accounted for Nu473.62 million. It is also evident that there is significant scope to upscale domestic pilgrimage as only 12% of domestic travel thus far has involved such travel.

Figure 7: Domestic and Outbound Tourism, 2019

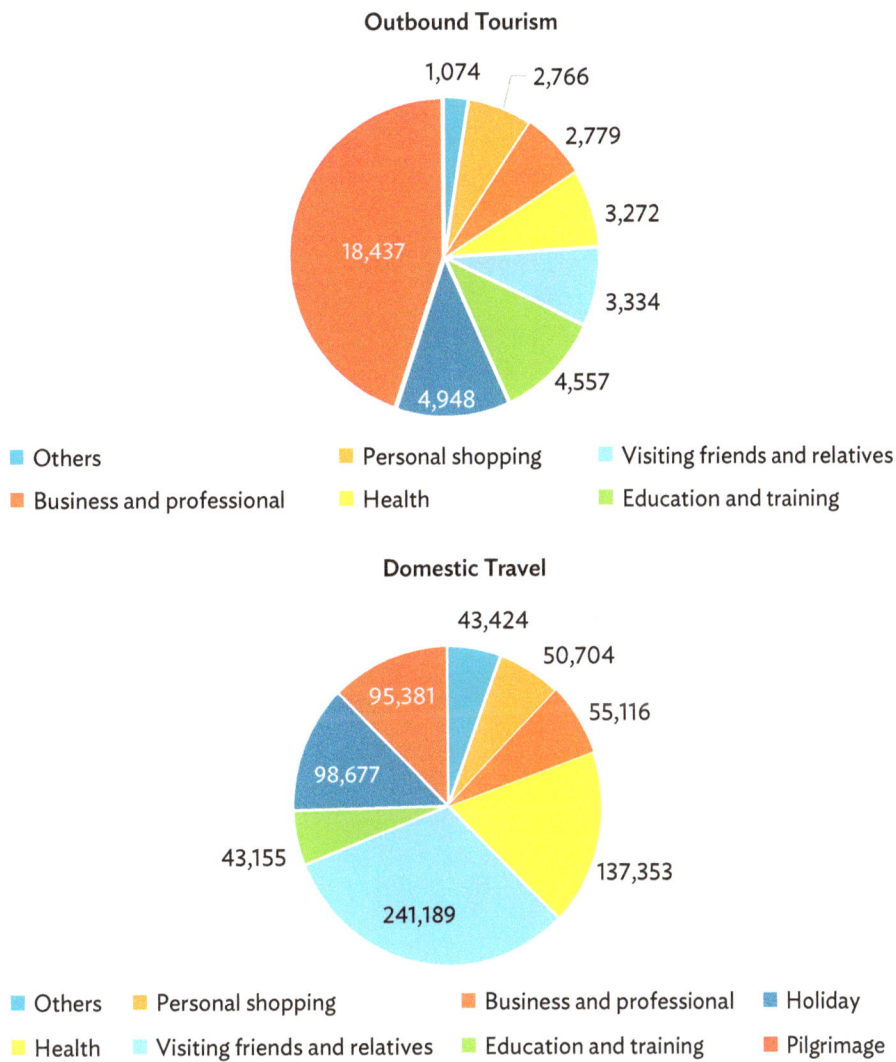

Outbound Tourism

- Others
- Business and professional
- Personal shopping
- Health
- Visiting friends and relatives
- Education and training

Domestic Travel

- Others
- Personal shopping
- Business and professional
- Holiday
- Health
- Visiting friends and relatives
- Education and training
- Pilgrimage

Source: Royal Government of Bhutan, Tourism Council of Bhutan. 2020. Domestic and Outbound Tourism Survey, 2019.

---

25   K. Dorji. 2015. Pilgrimage to BodhGaya: An Experience. *Kuensel*. 4 April. https://kuenselonline.com/pilgrimage-to-bodhgaya-an-experience/.

26   TCB. 2020. *Domestic and Outbound Tourism Survey, 2019*.

The TCB has been proactive by initiating the development of Druk Neykor, connecting 108 temples in the country. The Thimphu version, comprising 16 sites (temples and holy sites), was launched on 17 December 2020.[27] On the institutional front, guidelines for the Management of Domestic Tourism and the Domestic Tourism Promotion Strategy have been developed.

Beyond pilgrimage, additional scope for domestic tourism has been observed based on the growing number of locals going for hiking and glamping. More specifically, it is expected that the spending potential of those households who usually travel out of the country in the winter to destinations such as Bangkok can be explored. To facilitate this, "Druk Kora," a domestic tourism campaign featuring domestic tour packages offered by tour operators and other promoters, has been launched on the TCB's website. These will provide locals with potential activities and destinations to explore in the country and support local tourism businesses. The Food Map of Bhutan, developed by the Royal Institute for Tourism and Hospitality, is also intended to promote the culinary heritage of Bhutan.[28]

Bubble Tourism

A new form of tourism that has emerged is "Bubble Tourism." Under such an arrangement, a set of countries that have managed to contain the pandemic agree to open their borders to each other. Countries such as Fiji, Maldives, and Sri Lanka have already adopted such an arrangement. While the TCB has submitted a proposal for such an arrangement to the COVID-19 TAG, no decision has been taken yet.[29] A special arrangement has been reached only with India, though this is perhaps due to the close ties between the two countries and not necessarily targeted at promoting tourism.

The TCB proposes two possible options for bubble travel. The first is to undergo a quarantine period of 3 days, 7 days, or 14 days. Under the 3-day quarantine option, the tourist will have to present a COVID-19 test certificate taken 72 hours before flying to Bhutan. Upon entering Bhutan, they will be placed in quarantine at identified hotels. The TAG will have to decide on the duration. Following the quarantine duration, if they test negative, they will be eligible for a quarantine mode itinerary. To contain possible infection, the same vehicles and staff will be responsible, and tourists will have to stick to the pre-identified itinerary that includes places where there is no contact with the public. To keep tourists engaged, the TCB is also proposing activities such as wellness, meditation, and retreat during the quarantine.

Once a tourist completes 14 days, whether under quarantine or a quarantine-mode travel, they will be administered another test. If they test negative, the proposal is to allow them to move more freely with a normal itinerary.

The second option is to replace normal quarantine with a mode of travel that is carefully isolated. Once a tourist tests negative, they can go on special trekking programs and routes that are isolated and where they do not come into contact with locals. For instance, the Druk Path or the Snowman's Trek could be

---

[27] Royal Government of Bhutan, Tourism Council of Bhutan. 2021. *Bhutan Tourism Monitor 2020*. https://www.tourism.gov.bt/ uploads/attachment_files/tcb_K5Y19KXy_BHUTAN%20TOURISM%20MONITOR%202020.pdf.

[28] Y. Dorji. 2020. TCB Launches Three New Products To Promote Domestic Tourism. *Bhutan Broadcasting Service*. 17 December. http://www.bbs.bt/news/?p=140939.

[29] T. Lamzang. 2020. TCB to Introduce Bubble Tourism from March 2021. *The Bhutanese*. 5 September. https://thebhutanese.bt/ tcb-to-propose-bubble-tourism-from-march-2021/.

offered with no contact with locals. A variation of the non-quarantine option could include a 10-day isolated retreat program.

While these do offer some possible avenues to revive the sector, it is important to assess the capacity of the country in undertaking such a complex arrangement. In addition to competent industry professionals, this will also require the engagement of health personnel. Recent developments such as the second lockdown and the contagiousness of the new variants of the virus point to a protracted reopening and the possibility of accepting international tourists amid increasing global vaccination rates. The capacity of the health system to manage a full-blown outbreak is constrained by numerous factors such as the scarcity of personnel, especially doctors. Thus, the cost of the outbreak needs to be weighed against the possible benefits from bringing in a handful of tourists. It has been inferred that the source of the second outbreak is the Paro International Airport, highlighting the risks.[30]

30   T. Lamzang. 2021. How Complacency and Lax Protocols Led to the Nation's Second COVID-19 Outbreak. *The Bhutanese.* 10 January. https://thebhutanese.bt/how-complacency-and-lax-protocols-led-to-the-nations-second-covid-19-outbreak/.

VII Conclusion

Bhutan has demonstrated a proactive approach in implementing measures to contain the spread of COVID-19, including restrictions on tourists since March 2020. While these have resulted in effective containment, supply-side disruptions in the construction and manufacturing sectors have been exacerbated by a dampening of demand and, in some cases, a complete standstill in areas such as tourism. Given the limited resources and capacity to cope with a full-blown outbreak, such tradeoffs between preventive measures and economic activity were inevitable. Central to coping with the pandemic has been the swift and decisive interventions such as the social relief grants provided to the most affected people. Additional monetary and fiscal measures, including the interest waivers, have allowed businesses to remain solvent for now. However, the pandemic also presents a unique opportunity to pursue other initiatives that strengthen the economy's long-term potential. Such measures can be seen in the tourism sector's plan. The strategic thrust of the interventions for the sector are based on engaging economically displaced while initiating major reforms and investments for a stronger opening. The sector is also tapping into the underexplored domestic tourism segment, pilgrimages in particular, as an alternative. Other alternatives such as bubble tourism are also being explored, although the risks and possible benefits need to be assessed.

References

Asian Development Bank. Bhutan: COVID-19 Active Response and Expenditure Support Program. https://www.adb.org/projects/54183-001/main.

Dorji, K. 2015. Pilgrimage to BodhGaya: An Experience. *Kuensel.* 4 April. https://kuenselonline.com/pilgrimage-to-bodhgaya-an-experience/.

Dorji, Y. 2020. TCB Launches Three New Products To Promote Domestic Tourism. *Bhutan Broadcasting Service.* 17 December. http://www.bbs.bt/news/?p=140939.

Lamzang, T. 2020. TCB To Introduce Bubble Tourism From March 2021. *The Bhutanese.* 5 September. https://thebhutanese.bt/tcb-to-propose-bubble-tourism-from-march-2021/.

Lamzang, T. 2021. How Complacency and Lax Protocols Led to the Nation's Second COVID-19 Outbreak. *The Bhutanese.* 10 January. https://thebhutanese.bt/how-complacency-and-lax-protocols-led-to-the-nations-second-covid-19-outbreak/.

Lhaden, Y. 2021. Gender-Based Violence Spikes 53.5% in 2020. *Kuensel.*19 March. https://kuenselonline.com/gender-based-violence-spikes-53-5-percent-in-2020/.

Palden, T. 2020. Druk Gyalpo's Kidu Extended for the Most Needy. *Kuensel.* 25 December. https://kuenselonline.com/druk-gyalpos-reliefkidu-extended-for-the-most-needy/.

Royal Government of Bhutan. 2020. *Economic Contingency Plan—Redesigning Development: Attaining Greater Heights.* https://www.cabinet.gov.bt/wp-content/uploads/2020/07/ECP-2020.pdf.

Royal Government of Bhutan, Ministry of Finance. 2020. *National Budget Report 2020–2021.*

Royal Government of Bhutan, Ministry of Health. 2020. National Preparedness and Response Plan for Outbreak of Novel Coronavirus. Thimphu. 16 March. http://www.moh.gov.bt/wp-content/uploads/ict-files/2020/01/National-Preparedness-and-Response-Plan-4th-ed.pdf.

Royal Government of Bhutan, National Credit Guarantee Scheme. http://www.ncgs.gov.bt/.

Royal Government of Bhutan, National Statistics Bureau and United Nations Development Programme. 2020. *Rapid Socio-Economic Impact Assessment of COVID-19 on Bhutan's Tourism Sector: An Analysis of the Vulnerability of Individuals, Households and Businesses Engaged in the Tourism Sector.*

May. https://www.bt.undp.org/content/bhutan/en/home/library/environment_energy/rapid-socio-economic-impact-assessment-of-covid-19-on-bhutan-s-t.html.

Royal Government of Bhutan, Prime Minister's Office. 2020. State of the Nation Address.

Royal Government of Bhutan, Royal Monetary Authority. 2021. *Monthly Statistical Bulletin.* January. Thimphu.

Royal Government of Bhutan, Tourism Council of Bhutan. 2020. *Bhutan Tourism Monitor 2019.* Thimphu. https://www.tourism.gov.bt/uploads/attachment_files/tcb_TNiOKGow_BTM%202019.pdf.

Royal Government of Bhutan, Tourism Council of Bhutan. 2021. *Bhutan Tourism Monitor 2020.* https://www.tourism.gov.bt/uploads/attachment_files/tcb_K5Y19KXy_BHUTAN%20TOURISM%20 MONITOR%202020.pdf.

Royal Government of Bhutan, Tourism Council of Bhutan. 2020. *Domestic and Outbound Tourism Survey 2019.*

Royal Government of Bhutan, Tourism Council of Bhutan. 2020. *Tourism Levy Act of Bhutan.* Thimphu. https://www.tourism.gov.bt/uploads/attachment_files/tcb_pw9dDZzH_Tourism%20Levy%20 Act%20of%20Bhutan%202020.pdf.

Subba, M. B. 2021. Unprecendented Setbacks for Economy. *Kuensel.* 13 February. https://kuenselonline. com/unprecedentedsetbacks-for-economy/.

Tshedup, Y. 2020. Govt. To Set Up S/Jongkhar and Gelephu as Tourist Entry Points. *Kuensel.* 2 July. https://kuenselonline.com/govt-to-set-up-s-jongkhar-and-gelephu-as-tourist-entry-points/.

Tshering, L. 2020. *State of the Nation.* Fourth Session: The Third Parliament of Bhutan. 12 December. https://www.nab.gov.bt/assets/uploads/images/news/2020/State_of_the_Nation_2020.pdf.

World Health Organization. https://data.worldbank.org/ (accessed 8 January 2021).